Mental Health Stigma:

Investigating Social Stigmatization and Strategies
to Reduce It

Flawless Dave

Table of Contents

I. Introduction

Definition of Mental Health Stigma

Let's take a closer look at the fascinating topic of mental health stigma. We'll explore what it is, why it matters, and how it affects individuals. So, grab a cup of coffee, get comfortable, and let's embark on this enlightening journey together!

Mental health stigma is a concept that revolves around the negative attitudes, beliefs, and stereotypes people have towards those with mental health conditions. It is a pervasive issue that can create barriers, impede recovery, and perpetuate discrimination against those who are already dealing with the challenges of mental illness.

To gain a better understanding of mental health stigma, let's look at some examples that will help us gain a clearer picture.

Jane's Struggle with Depression

Imagine Jane, a vibrant young woman, who has been diagnosed with depression. She experiences intense sadness, loss of interest in activities she once loved, and struggles with daily tasks. Despite her best efforts to seek help, some people around her start to treat her differently. They may label her as lazy, weak, or attention-seeking, without fully understanding the complexities of depression. This judgmental behavior and lack of empathy from others represent the essence of mental health stigma.

John's Battle with Anxiety

Now, let's meet John, an ambitious professional who faces severe anxiety. His anxiety often leads to panic attacks and difficulty in social situations. Unfortunately, when John musters up the courage to disclose his condition to his employer, he encounters a dismissive response. His employer questions his capabilities, assumes he's unreliable, and refrains from offering necessary accommodations. This response reflects how mental health stigma can impact workplace environments and prevent individuals from seeking support.

These examples demonstrate the real-life consequences of mental health stigma. They showcase the judgment, misconceptions, and discrimination that individuals with mental health conditions may encounter on a daily basis. It is essential to recognize that mental health conditions are genuine health issues that deserve empathy, understanding, and appropriate support.

The effects of mental health stigma go beyond individual experiences. It permeates society, affecting families, communities, workplaces, and even healthcare systems. Stigma can discourage people from seeking professional help, leading to delayed or inadequate treatment. It also contributes to the silence surrounding mental health, making it difficult to have open conversations and reduce the associated shame and isolation.

But, there is hope! Raising awareness, challenging stereotypes, and promoting understanding can help break down the walls of mental health stigma.

Overview of Mental Health Stigma

Mental health stigma is a pervasive issue that revolves around the negative attitudes, beliefs, and stereotypes society holds towards individuals with mental health conditions. It's like a dark cloud that hangs over people's understanding of mental illness, making it difficult for those affected to be seen and heard without judgment or prejudice. To better comprehend this concept, let's look at some case studies that will bring it to life.

Take Sarah, a creative and talented artist living with bipolar disorder. She experiences alternating episodes of extreme highs (mania) and lows (depression). Despite her incredible artistic abilities, Sarah faces barriers when trying to share her work or pursue opportunities. People may disregard her talent, attributing her creations solely to her mental illness, without recognizing her individuality and artistic merit. This disregard for her abilities is a direct result of mental health stigma.

Then there's Mark, a compassionate and intelligent young man diagnosed with schizophrenia. He experiences hallucinations and delusions, which can be distressing and disorienting. Unfortunately, due to the portrayal of schizophrenia in popular media as violent or dangerous,

Mark faces significant discrimination and fear from others. This societal fear leads to isolation and hinders his ability to build meaningful connections and engage fully in society.

These examples demonstrate the real-life impact of mental health stigma. Preconceived notions, stereotypes, and a lack of understanding can marginalize individuals and limit their opportunities for growth and inclusion. The effects of mental health stigma ripple throughout various aspects of life, from healthcare to education, employment, and social relationships. Additionally, the fear and shame associated with mental health stigma prevent many individuals from seeking help.

However, there is hope. Advocacy movements, educational initiatives, and brave individuals sharing their stories have sparked conversations and begun dismantling the walls of stigma.

II. Causes of Mental Health Stigma

Historical Context

Exploring the history of mental health stigma can help us gain insight into why it still exists today. Let's take a journey together and uncover the various factors that have contributed to the development of this issue.

Throughout the ages, societies have held various beliefs and perceptions about mental health, often rooted in fear, ignorance, and cultural norms. These attitudes have had a significant impact on the stigma we experience today.

For example, in ancient times, mental health conditions were often attributed to supernatural causes. People believed that individuals with mental illnesses were possessed by evil spirits, cursed, or under the influence of witchcraft. This led to the social exclusion and mistreatment of those affected, as well as the notion that those with mental health challenges were dangerous or morally corrupt.

The 17th to 19th centuries saw the rise of institutionalization in asylums. These facilities were intended to provide care for individuals with mental illness, but they often became overcrowded, unsanitary, and inhumane. Asylums were isolated from society, and people with mental health conditions were stigmatized as "mad" or "insane," further reinforcing the idea that mental illness was something to be hidden away and treated as a source of shame.

The late 19th and early 20th centuries saw the rise of eugenics and social Darwinism, which further fueled mental health stigma. These ideologies promoted the idea of "survival of the fittest" and attempted to improve the genetic quality of the human population. People with mental illnesses were often considered "defective" or "inferior" and were subjected to forced sterilization, exclusion from society, or even euthanasia. These practices only served to reinforce the belief that individuals with mental health conditions were undesirable and perpetuate stigma.

These examples demonstrate how deeply rooted and ingrained these stigmatizing attitudes can be. While we have come a long way in our understanding of mental health, remnants of these historical stigmas still persist today. Media portrayals, language used in everyday conversations, and even subtle biases can all contribute to negative stereotypes and the marginalization of those with mental health conditions.

It is essential to recognize the historical context of mental health stigma in order to understand why it persists and the importance of challenging it. By gaining awareness of the origins of stigma, we can actively work towards creating a more compassionate and inclusive society, free from the burdens of historical prejudices.

Cultural Factors

Culture is a broad concept that encompasses a variety of factors, such as societal norms, religious beliefs, language, and traditions. These elements can have a major impact on how mental health is perceived and understood within a particular community or society.

Collectivism and Stigma

In cultures that prioritize collective values, where the needs of the group come before individual needs, mental health issues can be seen as a sign of weakness or a burden on the community. As a result, people may be reluctant to talk about their struggles, fearing rejection or stigmatization from their own community.

Religious and Spiritual Beliefs

Religious and spiritual beliefs also have a major influence on attitudes towards mental health. In some cultures, mental health conditions such as schizophrenia or bipolar disorder may be attributed to spiritual afflictions rather than medical explanations. This can lead to a lack of understanding and support from religious communities.

Language and Stigmatizing Terminology

Language is a powerful cultural factor that can perpetuate stigma. Certain derogatory terms and expressions related to mental health are deeply embedded in our vernacular. For example, using words like "crazy," "psycho," or "lunatic" in casual conversations can reinforce negative stereotypes and contribute to the marginalization of individuals with mental health conditions. It is important to use language that is respectful, inclusive, and person-centered.

These cultural factors demonstrate how societal norms, religious beliefs, and language can shape the perception of mental health and contribute to stigma. They emphasize the importance of cultural competence and understanding in effectively addressing mental health stigma.

It is essential to recognize that cultural factors vary across different communities and societies. While some cultures may openly stigmatize mental health, others may have more subtle forms of stigma. Understanding and respecting diverse cultural perspectives is essential in tackling mental health stigma in a comprehensive manner.

Media Representation

Media representation has the potential to shape our understanding of mental health conditions. Unfortunately, it often reinforces negative stereotypes and stigma. Let's explore how media can influence our perceptions and attitudes towards mental health.

For example, characters with mental health conditions are often portrayed as violent or dangerous in movies and TV shows. This creates a distorted image and contributes to the public's fear and misunderstanding of individuals with mental illnesses. By associating mental health with violence, media representations can perpetuate the stigmatizing notion that people with mental health conditions are unpredictable or prone to harm others.

News outlets can also sensationalize stories related to mental health, focusing on extreme or rare cases. This sensationalism can lead to generalizations and misconceptions about mental health conditions. It can create an environment where individuals with mental illnesses are seen as outliers or anomalies, further perpetuating stigma and making it difficult for people to seek help without fear of judgment or scrutiny.

Social media can also be a breeding ground for stigmatizing language and stereotypes related to mental health. Memes, jokes, and derogatory terms often circulate, reinforcing negative attitudes and perpetuating stigma. This casual use of stigmatizing language normalizes the marginalization of individuals with mental health conditions and inhibits open conversations about mental health.

These examples demonstrate how media representation can contribute to mental health stigma by distorting perceptions, reinforcing stereotypes, and sensationalizing stories. It's important to note that not all media representations are stigmatizing, and some platforms and creators are actively working to challenge stigma and promote understanding. However, the prevalence of stigmatizing portrayals in mainstream media highlights the need for critical media literacy and responsible representation.

We can all play a role in combating stigma by advocating for accurate and sensitive portrayals of mental health in the media. Promoting diverse and authentic narratives, featuring individuals with lived experiences, and showcasing stories of recovery and resilience can help reshape public perceptions and challenge stigmatizing beliefs. As consumers of media, we can also critically analyze and engage with media content. By actively challenging stigmatizing representations, supporting positive and accurate portrayals, and promoting open conversations about mental health, we can be catalysts for change.

III. Effects of Mental Health Stigma

Impact on Mental Health

Mental health stigma can have a far-reaching and devastating impact on individuals, families, and communities. It can lead to self-stigma and internalized shame, create barriers to seeking help, cause social isolation and a lack of support, and even lead to employment and educational challenges. Furthermore, it can impede individuals' progress in treatment and recovery processes.

Self-stigma and internalized shame can erode individuals' self-esteem, confidence, and overall sense of identity, making it even more difficult to seek help and engage in effective treatment. The fear of being judged or labeled can prevent individuals from reaching out to mental health professionals or disclosing their struggles to friends and family, prolonging their suffering and delaying appropriate treatment.

Stigma can also lead to social isolation and a lack of support from friends, family, and communities. People may distance themselves from individuals with mental health conditions due to fear, misunderstanding, or discomfort, intensifying feelings of loneliness and contributing to a lack of understanding.

Mental health stigma can also have a significant impact on individuals' educational and occupational experiences. Discrimination and bias in the workplace and educational institutions can limit opportunities for growth, advancement, and fair treatment. People may face reduced job prospects, discrimination during hiring processes, or difficulties in academic settings, leading to increased stress, financial strain, and a sense of hopelessness.

Finally, stigma can have a profound impact on individuals' adherence to treatment and recovery processes. The fear of judgment or being labeled as "mentally ill" can deter individuals from taking medication, attending therapy sessions, or engaging in other necessary forms of treatment, hindering their progress and recovery.

It's essential to recognize that mental health stigma doesn't just affect individuals—it affects families, communities, and society as a whole. The collective silence and lack of understanding surrounding mental health can prevent open conversations, limit resources, and perpetuate a culture of shame and discrimination.

Barriers to Seeking Help

Mental health stigma can be incredibly isolating and can erect walls that make it difficult for individuals to reach out and access the support they need.

One of the most significant obstacles is the fear of being judged or labeled. People may worry that seeking help for mental health issues will lead to others perceiving them differently or thinking they are "weak" or "crazy." This fear can be paralyzing and stop individuals from confiding in others, seeking professional help, or getting the treatment they need.

Stigma can also lead to self-stigmatization, where individuals internalize negative beliefs about themselves and their mental health condition. This can cause feelings of shame, guilt, or a sense of personal failure, making it even harder to acknowledge that they need assistance.

A lack of awareness and understanding about mental health can also be a barrier. Misconceptions and stereotypes can lead to people trivializing individuals' struggles or suggesting that their mental health challenges are not serious enough to warrant help. This can be incredibly discouraging and make it difficult to seek support.

In addition, stigma can contribute to limited access to mental health resources and services. In some communities, mental health services may be scarce, inadequate, or stigmatized themselves. This can make it even harder for individuals to get the help they need.

Finally, intersectionality plays a key role in understanding the barriers faced by marginalized groups. People from racial or ethnic minority backgrounds, LGBTQ+ individuals, or those with disabilities may experience additional layers of stigma and discrimination, making it even more challenging to access the mental health system.

It's important to break down these barriers and create an environment where individuals feel safe to seek help. This involves fostering understanding, promoting empathy, and raising awareness about mental health. Mental health professionals, community organizations, and policy makers also have a role to play in removing barriers to seeking help, such as developing culturally sensitive services, increasing mental health education, and challenging stigma at the systemic level.

IV. Strategies to Reduce Mental Health Stigma

Education and Awareness

Let's take a look at some of the key ways to combat mental health stigma: education and awareness. By increasing our knowledge and understanding of mental health, we can challenge stigmatizing beliefs and create a more supportive society.

Educating ourselves on mental health is a great way to reduce stigma. By providing accurate information about different conditions, their causes, and available treatments, we can debunk any false beliefs. We can also learn that mental illnesses are medical conditions caused by a combination of genetic, biological, and environmental factors, rather than personal weakness or character flaws.

Sharing personal stories and lived experiences is another powerful way to foster empathy and understanding. When individuals with mental health conditions share their journeys, challenges, and triumphs, it helps us relate on a personal level. These stories break down barriers, challenge stereotypes, and show that anyone can be affected by mental health issues.

Integrating mental health literacy into educational curricula is also important for nurturing understanding and empathy from a young age. By teaching children and adolescents about mental health, the importance of self-care, and how to support others, we can create a foundation of empathy and acceptance.

Public awareness campaigns are also pivotal in reaching broader audiences and challenging mental health stigma. These campaigns utilize various media platforms, such as television, social media, and community events, to disseminate accurate information, promote understanding, and encourage help-seeking behavior.

Finally, educating healthcare providers and professionals is essential in reducing stigma within healthcare settings. By providing training on mental health, the impact of stigma, and promoting culturally sensitive practices, professionals can ensure that individuals receive respectful and person-centered care.

These strategies help us foster empathy, challenge stereotypes, and promote open conversations about mental health. Ultimately, they contribute to a more inclusive and supportive environment for individuals with mental health conditions.

Normalizing Mental Health Conversations

Normalizing conversations about mental health means making it a regular part of our everyday lives. It involves breaking the silence, challenging the taboo, and creating a safe space for open dialogue. There are many ways to do this, such as sharing personal experiences, using social media and online communities, incorporating media representation, implementing workplace initiatives, and educating in schools.

Sharing personal stories can help humanize the experience, reduce feelings of isolation, and create an atmosphere of understanding and empathy. Social media and online platforms provide a space for individuals to connect, support one another, and engage in discussions without fear of judgment. Media representation that portrays mental health experiences authentically and sensitively can spark conversations and encourage viewers to reflect on their own well-being.

At work, employers can implement initiatives such as mental health training, employee resource groups, and dedicated support systems. This helps employees feel supported, reduces stigma, and fosters a culture of well-being. In schools, integrating mental health education into the curriculum, providing resources for students, and promoting peer support systems can create an environment where mental health is discussed openly and without judgment.

These conversations empower individuals to speak up, seek support, and prioritize their well-being. They contribute to a society where mental health is viewed as an integral part of overall health and where seeking help is seen as a sign of strength.

Promoting Positive Representation

Creating a more inclusive and accepting society starts with promoting positive representation of mental health. This involves portraying mental health experiences in a realistic, respectful, and empathetic manner. By showcasing diverse stories and characters, we can challenge stigmatizing narratives, humanize the experiences of individuals with mental health conditions, and foster understanding.

Authentic portrayals in media, such as movies, TV shows, and literature, can play a powerful role in shaping public perceptions of mental health. It is important to depict mental health experiences in an authentic and nuanced way. For example, a TV series that realistically portrays a character with depression, depicting their daily struggles, treatment journey, and relationships, can help viewers develop a deeper understanding of the condition and challenge stigmatizing beliefs.

Personal testimonies and lived experiences can also have a profound impact on reducing stigma. By sharing diverse stories of individuals with mental health conditions, we can humanize the experiences and foster empathy. These stories can come from various platforms, such as public speaking events, podcasts, books, or online platforms. When people hear firsthand accounts of others' challenges, resilience, and recovery, it helps break down barriers and encourages a more compassionate view of mental health.

Art and creativity offer unique avenues for promoting positive representation. Artists can use their work to explore mental health themes, challenge stereotypes, and create thought-provoking pieces that encourage dialogue. Art exhibits, photography, poetry, and music can all serve as platforms to showcase the diverse experiences of mental health and provide opportunities for reflection and empathy.

It is also important to amplify diverse voices and perspectives. This involves ensuring that individuals from different backgrounds, cultures, and identities are included in discussions about mental health. For instance, highlighting the experiences of marginalized communities or LGBTQ+ individuals can shed light on the unique challenges they face and contribute to a more inclusive understanding of mental health.

Finally, public figures, celebrities, and influencers have the power to shape public opinion and challenge stigma. When well-known individuals openly discuss their mental health journeys, it helps normalize these conversations and encourages others to seek support. By sharing their stories, public figures can inspire hope, break down barriers, and create a sense of unity in the face of mental health challenges.

By promoting positive representation of mental health, we can help dismantle stigmatizing beliefs and foster a more inclusive and accepting society. Showcasing diverse experiences, challenging stereotypes, and highlighting the strengths and resilience of individuals with mental health conditions can create an environment that values and supports everyone's mental well-being.

V. Conclusion

Summary of Mental Health Stigma

It is essential to understand the nature and effects of mental health stigma in order to create a more inclusive and compassionate society. Let's review the key points from our enlightening discussion! Mental health stigma is the negative beliefs, stereotypes, and prejudices that surround mental health conditions. It can lead to social marginalization, discrimination, and lack of understanding for those with mental health issues. This stigma has a deep impact on individuals' emotional, psychological, and social well-being, and can even have broader societal implications. Stigma has its roots in ancient supernatural beliefs, the era of institutionalization, and the rise of eugenics and social Darwinism. Cultural factors, such as collectivism, religious beliefs, and stigmatizing language, also contribute to stigma. Media representation also plays a role in perpetuating stigma. To reduce stigma, education and awareness, normalizing mental health conversations, and promoting positive representation are all strategies that can be employed. These strategies work together to reduce stigma and create a supportive environment.

Summary of Strategies to Reduce Mental Health Stigma

Let's take a moment to review the strategies we've discussed to combat mental health stigma. By implementing these approaches, we can create a more supportive environment for individuals with mental health conditions and challenge the stigma that surrounds them. So, let's recap these strategies together!

Education and Awareness:

Educating ourselves and others is a powerful tool in reducing stigma. By promoting accurate information, dispelling myths, and raising awareness about mental health, we can challenge misconceptions and foster understanding. We can do this through educational initiatives, mental health literacy in schools, and public awareness campaigns.

Normalizing Mental Health Conversations:

Normalizing mental health conversations involves breaking the silence and creating a safe space for open dialogue. We can do this by sharing personal experiences, leveraging social media, promoting media representation, implementing workplace initiatives, and integrating mental health education in schools. These discussions help individuals feel supported, reduce stigma, and empower them to seek help when needed.

Promoting positive representation is about showcasing diverse and authentic portrayals of mental health experiences. We can do this by highlighting personal testimonies, diverse voices, and accurate media representations. This helps to challenge stigmatizing narratives, humanize the experiences of individuals with mental health conditions, and foster empathy. Through art, creativity, and the stories of role models, we can create a more inclusive understanding of mental health.

Education and awareness provide the foundation for understanding, normalizing mental health conversations creates an environment of acceptance, and promoting positive representation challenges stigma and fosters empathy.

It's important to remember that reducing mental health stigma is a collective effort. We can all play a role in challenging stigmatizing beliefs, supporting those affected by mental health conditions, and creating inclusive communities. Every conversation, every act of empathy, and every step taken toward understanding contributes to a society where mental health is embraced and respected.

Mental health stigma is a pervasive issue that has a wide-reaching impact on individuals, families, communities, and society as a whole. It can be a barrier to seeking help, perpetuate misunderstandings, and lead to the marginalization of those with mental health conditions. To combat this, we have explored a range of strategies to create a more inclusive and supportive environment.

Education and awareness are powerful tools. By challenging stigmatizing beliefs, providing accurate information, and promoting understanding, we can break down the walls of ignorance and foster empathy and acceptance. Additionally, normalizing mental health conversations is essential. By sharing our stories, leveraging social media, and fostering open dialogue, we can create safe spaces for individuals to seek support and know that they are not alone.

Positive representation is also key. By showcasing diverse and authentic portrayals of mental health, we can challenge stereotypes, humanize experiences, and foster empathy. Whether through media, art, or personal testimonies, we can create a more inclusive understanding of mental health.

Combating mental health stigma is a collective effort. It requires each of us to play a role—whether as individuals, communities, or society at large. Small actions like using respectful language, offering support, and being a compassionate listener can make a big difference.

Let's carry the spirit of empathy, understanding, and support in our daily lives. Let's continue to challenge stigma, promote open conversations, and create environments where mental health is accepted, understood, and prioritized. Together, we can build a world where mental health is destigmatized, where individuals feel safe to seek help, and where empathy and compassion are the norm. Your voice, your actions, and your support all matter.

www.ingramcontent.com/pod-product-compliance
Lightning Source LLC
Chambersburg PA
CBHW060911260726
48661CB00008B/3577